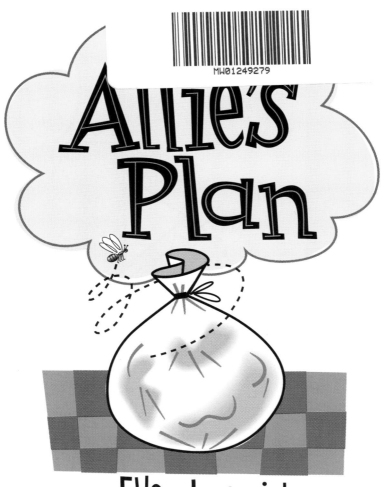

Allie's Plan

by Ellen Javernick
illustrated by Eric Larsen

MODERN CURRICULUM PRESS
Pearson Learning Group

Allie wanted to shout,

2

3

Allie covered her nose.
"Sometimes it smells!" she said.

5

6

"I don't want to do this job," she complained.

"We all have jobs, Allie," said Dad.

"You take out the trash.
Andy walks the dog."

"Working together is what a family is all about."

"Get your job done. Then you can play," said Dad.

"Wait!" said Allie. "I have a great plan!"

"I think this will work," said Dad. "We will make a chart."

The Chores

	Sun.	Mon.	Tues.	Weds.	Thur.	Fri.	Sat.
Mom	Dishes	Floor	Trash	Dog	Dishes	Floor	Trash
Dad	Floor	Trash	Dog	Dishes	Floor	Trash	Dog
Allie	Trash	Dog	Dishes	Floor	Trash	Dog	Dishes
Andy	Dog	Dishes	Floor	Trash	Dog	Dishes	Floor

Hi!